THEOLOGY OF BIBLICAL LEADERSHIP

THEOLOGY OF BIBLICAL LEADERSHIP

PASTOR RONELLE J MCGRAW JR, ThM

XULON PRESS

Xulon Press
2301 Lucien Way #415
Maitland, FL 32751
407.339.4217
www.xulonpress.com

PRESS

Unless otherwise indicated, Scripture quotations taken from the King James Version (KJV) – *public domain.*

Scripture quotations taken from the Holy Bible, New International Version (NIV). Copyright © 1973, 1978, 1984, 2011 by Biblica, Inc.™. Used by permission. All rights reserved.

Paperback ISBN-13: 978-1-66286-665-4
Ebook ISBN-13: 978-1-66286-666-1

TABLE OF CONTENTS

Servant Leaders 1

Ethical Motivations in the Leader 13

Decision Making 25

Conflicts 31

Conflict Resolution 37

Salvaging a Confrontation Ambush 43

The Making of a Good Leader 47

The Spiritual Lifestyle of a Leader 57

Conclusion 59

References 61

SERVANT LEADERS

My preaching career began in June of 1987 at my home church—Tolliver Temple Church of God In Christ—located in Seattle, Washington. I was only nineteen years of age at the time. Having given my life to the Lord a little over a year before, I knew my purpose; God called me to preach His Word. But like most people who are called, I did not want to comply.

When I first began preaching, there was not a theological seminary that I wanted to attend in the local area. The only resources available for me to learn to preach God's Word were the Bible, attending Sunday School, being active in the Bible Band, and YPWW.

I served ten years as assistant pastor from 1995 to 2005 under the direction of my father, Superintendent Ronelle McGraw Sr. During that time, I was prepared for my current position. I currently hold the position as Pastor of Praise Chapel Church of God in Christ. I acquired this position after my father unexpectedly went home to be with the Lord.

On Thanksgiving Day in 2005, my father passed into glory. At that moment, I became the Pastor of Praise Chapel Church of God in Christ. I felt as though my whole world had ended, and the weight of the church and my family was now on my shoulders. My father and pastor were no longer here on Earth with me. What was I going to do? There was no time to grieve, not a moment to cry. I had to rise to the occasion that Sunday and deliver a message of hope when I was grieving on the inside. I had to recall all of the training I had received from my father who was not only a phenomenal pastor but a great leader. I had to put everything I had learned into practice. I exhibited leadership skills that I would go on to utilize during my tenure.

He consistently stressed the importance of accepting people wherever they may be in their life journey. He reminded me that leadership was not being Lord over God's people but to love them.

Neither as being lords over God's heritage but being examples to the flock. And when the chief Shepherd shall appear, ye shall receive a crown of glory that fadeth not away. Likewise, ye younger, submit yourselves unto the elder. Yea, all of you be subject one to another, and be clothed with humility: for God resisteth the proud, and giveth grace to the humble. (King James Version, 1989, 1 Peter 5:3-5)

The vision and mission statement of Praise Chapel is "To bring people of all nationalities to Christ that they might grow to Christ-like maturity." My father lived by this vision in his daily life so much so that it was within his spirit, but I questioned if it was in mine. Could I walk in the vision of the church on a consistent daily basis? Would I have a spirit that would amount to the spirt of my father's? I had nothing but questions, many of which could not be answered. During these times of uncertainty, Paul's letter to the Galatians quickly came to mind.

To glorify God with the fruit which we bear according to the fruit of the Spirit [which] is love, joy, peace, longsuffering, gentleness, goodness, faith, meekness, temperance: against such there is no law. And they that are Christ's have crucified the flesh with the affections and lusts. If we live in the Spirit, let us also walk in the Spirit. (King James Version, 1989, Galatians 5:22-26)

I had to build confidence and trust in my own spirit. I was groomed to fulfill this position, and I had to fulfill my duties to the best of my ability. Although I had been trained for many years, when the opportunity to rise to the occasion came, uncertainty overwhelmed me. As I can now report, I am truly living up to the expectations I believe my father aligned for me.

As I hold the pastoral position now, I am thankful for the opportunities and growth obtained during my years of service as an assistant pastor and the quick roll change. I found myself putting what I learned into practice and recollecting the statements that the apostle Paul scattered throughout his letters. "Therefore, I urge you to imitate me" (King James Version, 1989, I Corinthians 4:16). "Follow my example, as I follow the example of Christ" (King James Version, 1989, I Corinthians 11:1). "Join together in following my example, brothers and sisters, and just as you have us a model, keep your eyes on those who live as we do" (King James Version, 1989, Philippians 3:17). "Whatever you have learned or received or heard from me or seen in me put into practice" (King James Version, 1989, Philippians 4:9). "You became imitators of us and of the Lord" (King James Version, 1989, I Thessalonians 1:6). "For you yourself know How you ought to follow our example" (King James Version, 1989, II Thessalonians 3:17).

By following my father and studying about the apostle Paul, I found that Paul's leadership style was apparent. Paul says phrases like: Follow my example; Imitate me; Put what you learned into practice. The best way to lead is not to tell people what to do but to show them by example, and showing involves more than just a training session. One's complete lifestyle exemplifies what matters most in life. My father's life was an example of integrity, responsibility, investment, and empowerment.

Finding leaders who have integrity sometimes seems impossible. Godly leaders are those who we look to for example of good leadership. Paul's states, "You know how we lived among you, modeling integrity in every way. Far from taking advantage of them." Paul and his fellow missionaries were like parents to the Thessalonian believers, training and caring for them. They shared with the Thessalonians not only their message but also their very lives. This was because, like us, they were accountable to God.

Integrity is among the most important traits for a good leader to model. Followers can sense hypocrisy a mile away. "Do as I say, not as I do," does not inspire transformed lives or motivated action. One's confidence in us is not only judged by our words but by our actions, especially being in the position as a pastor. A leader must model responsibility and competence to their congregation to ensure that they have skills necessary to fulfill the responsibilities of a pastor.

Modeling responsibility is important because it demonstrates as leaders that we are not lazy and are always pushing forward to achieve our goals as an individual and pastor for the growth of the church. As a pastor, husband, and father I truly understand the importance of working and taking care of one's responsibilities.

While being in this position as pastor, the biggest complaint or concern from members is that they experienced many leaders not modeling responsibility. Some pastors did not ensure that their families and the church that they were pastoring were being taken care of in the proper way. Not only do I hear this complaint from new members in my own congregation but also from other members amongst the different congregations that I oversee. Like my father, I have become, in my opinion, a stand-up leader. I now also hold the position of District Superintendent, and many of the local pastors and their members confide in me.

There are many leaders who plan (and do) maintain their nine to five job until their church can compensate them financially. Concern and awareness for the financial and spiritual needs of the membership can take a toll on a pastor. The lack of a pastor modeling responsibility toward the family and the church membership can and will impact the church negatively by resulting in a lack of faith and spiritual maturity amongst the members.

We see in Thessalonians 1 and 2, Paul gives praise to the believers for their faith and spiritual maturity. The church was growing and thriving, but Paul would often tell certain members of the community to stop being lazy and get back to work. Paul particularly expresses the following sentiment: "And that ye study to be quiet, and to do your own business, and to work with your own hands, as we commanded you. That ye may walk honestly toward them that are without, and that ye may have lack of nothing" (King James Version, 1989, I Thessalonians 4:11-12).

Paul does not just give orders, but he points to his own example saying, "For you yourself know how you ought to follow our example." Paul reminds the Thessalonians that he was not lazy when he was with them, nor did he eat anyone's food without paying for it. Paul states that he and his companions worked night and day, laboring so that they would not be a burden to any of them. Like Paul, I understand the importance of working and being a servant leader. I have been modeling responsibility by not being a lazy leader and allowing my life to speak for itself.

However, Paul goes so far as to say that if someone refuses to work, they should not be allowed to eat. He explains, "For even when we were with you, this we commanded you, that if any would not work, neither should he eat" (2 Thessalonians 3:10). He goes on, "For ye remember, brethren, our labour and travail: for labouring night and day, because we would not be chargeable unto any of you, we preached unto you the gospel of God" (I Thessalonians 2:9).

As a full-time pastor of the gospel, like Paul, I could have lived off the support of others, but instead, I took responsibility for my own financial support – which I acknowledge not every pastor can do. If we as leaders expect others to fulfill their responsibilities, we need to go above and beyond in our own duties and responsibilities. "Be ye followers of me, even as I also am of Christ" (I Corinthians 11:1). In this verse, Paul again emphasizes his modeling leadership style. Every great leader can model excellent leadership by being a great example. People will follow your leadership if you are following the example of Christ. Leaders inspire others when they demonstrate true commitment to and investment in a shared vision. Consider a pastor who might mortgage their own home or cash in their retirement to launch a church or the CEO who takes a reduction in salary to avoid laying off loyal workers during COVID-19. Such actions may be risky, but they model commitment and investment. Following and modeling these traits relates not only to a leader's personal integrity, responsibility, and investment, but also to the task of leadership training itself by reproducing yourself in others.

My father was training me, but he was really reproducing himself back into me to become the husband, father, grandfather, and pastor I am today.

When Jesus chose twelve of his follows to be his inner circle of disciples, he called them simply to be with him. "And he ordained twelve, that they should be with him, and that he might send them forth to preach" (Mark 3:14). Jesus' followers were to learn by living with him and watching his example. I can recall growing up watching my parents singing and preaching the gospel, the sick being healed, and demons being cast out. I had not known or understood at the time that they were instilling in me what was needed for the season I am in today. Likewise, Christ sent out the disciples to replicate his ministry. "And to have power to heal sicknesses, and to cast out devils" (Mark 3:15).

In other words, Jesus reproduced himself in them so they would reproduce themselves in others. This is all true in the Great Commission, where Jesus' last instructions to his disciples are to make disciples of all nations.

And Jesus came and spoke unto them, saying, all power is given unto me in heaven and in earth. Go ye therefore, and teach all nations, baptizing them in the name of the Father, and of the Son, and of the Holy Ghost: Teaching them to observe all things whatsoever, I have commanded you: and, lo, I am with you always, even unto the end of the world. Amen. (Mark 28:18-20)

As disciples, they were to make disciples, reproducing themselves in others. Every good leader has the same responsibility as the disciples did to reproduce themselves in others. If this would truly take place in every church, we would not face the issue of continuing the ministry because the pastor was unable to fulfill his or her duties because of illness or death.

Paul used the same example for spiritual replication. He makes this clear in his letter, known to us as 2 Timothy, in which he instructs his assistant Timothy to carry on the task of leadership training after he is gone. Like Timothy, I was given specific instructions to carry out from my father who knew that he did not have much time left on this earth. My father reminded me of the things I have heard in the presence of many witnesses and those who are reliable members within our church community qualified to work in ministry with me. "And the things that thou hast heard of me among many witnesses, the same commit thou to faithful men, who shall be able to teach others also" (2 Timothy 2:2).

My father has replicated his ministry in me, and he expected me to do the same in others. A leader's primary role is to work him or herself out of a job by equipping and empowering others to utilize the gifts and abilities they have been given. A pastor is successful when the members of the congregation grow to Christ-like maturity. A CEO is successful when workers are effective and satisfied with the jobs that they perform daily.

A notably successful pastor requires training in equipping others to meet the expected demands of their roles, delegation of responsibilities, accountability, and empowerment. This was Jesus' way of equipping his followers. He trained the disciples by being a sound example of true servant leadership during his ministry.

He delegated responsibility and held them accountable by sending them out to preach and heal and by using the Great Commission as their guide. He empowered them with the Holy Ghost saying:

> If ye love me, keep my commandments. And I will pray the Father, and he shall give you another Comforter, that he may abide with you forever; Even the Spirit of truth; whom the world cannot receive, because it seeth him not, neither knoweth him: but ye know him; for he dwelleth with you, and shall be in you. I will not leave you comfortless: I will come to you. Yet a little while, and the world seeth me no more; but ye see me: because I live, ye shall live also. At that day ye shall know that I am in my Father, and ye in me, and I in you.[21] He that hath

my commandments, and keepeth them, he it is that loveth me: and he that loveth me shall be loved of my Father, and I will love him, and will manifest myself to him. Judas saith unto him, not Iscariot, Lord, how is it that thou wilt manifest thyself unto us, and not unto the world? Jesus answered and said unto him, If a man love me, he will keep my words: and my Father will love him, and we will come unto him, and make our abode with him. He that loveth me not keepeth not my sayings: and the word which ye hear is not mine, but the Father's which sent me. These things have I spoken unto you, being yet present with you.[26] But the Comforter, which is the Holy Ghost, whom the Father will send in my name, he shall teach you all things, and bring all things to your remembrance, whatsoever I have said unto you. Peace I leave with you, my peace I give unto you: not as the world giveth, give I unto you. Let not your heart be troubled, neither let it be afraid. Ye have heard how I said unto you, I go away, and come again unto you. If ye loved me, ye would rejoice, because I said, I go unto the Father: for my Father is greater than I. And now I have told you before it come to pass, that, when it is come to pass, ye might believe. Hereafter I will not talk much with you: for the prince of this world cometh, and hath nothing in me. But that the world may know that I love the Father; and as the Father gave me commandment, even so I do. Arise, let us go hence. (John 14:15-31)

Robert Greenleaf is often credited for initiating the current interest in servant leadership. Robert Greenleaf (1977) saw business leaders as needing to serve society more constructively than by merely increasing profits for the company. He felt business existed to provide meaningful work to their employees and, as it exists, to provide a product or service to the customer.

The philosophy of leading by serving includes building an environment that not only serves the needs of the organization but also provides a climate for its workers to grow and develop as human beings. After much research, Delphi method, Laub (1999) was developed as a functional definition of servant leaders and servant-led organizations.

Servant leaders and servant-led organizations value people by listening receptively, serving the needs of others first, and trusting people. This method allows for the opportunity to develop individuals by providing them opportunities for learning, modeling appropriate behavior, and building up others through encouragement. Servant leadership also allows for the opportunity to build a community by creating strong relationships, the opportunity to work collaboratively, and the ability to value individual difference. This method also allows for displays of authenticity by integrity, trust, openness, accountability, and a willingness to learn from others. Other attributes of this method are the ability to provide leadership by envisioning the future, taking initiative, and clarifying goals. One can share leadership roles to create a shared vision, guidelines for decision making, and the power to do so along with sharing status and increased responsibility at all levels of the organization.

The alternative leadership style to servant and servant-led is transformational leadership. The two have many parallels, but the distinct difference is the leader's focus. Transformational leaders build commitment and follow the organizational objectives, with the focus being the organization. A servant leader's highest value is the people, and organizational results are secondary.

The success of a servant leadership style is not based upon the results but the behavioral results of those who are under the leadership of a servant-led direction. Servant leadership remains an intuitive theory because little empirical evidence of servant leader behavior exists. The term servant leadership appears to be more than the sum of the words "service" and "leadership." The concept continues to be influential in the future, especially in the leadership of learning organizations.

Servant leadership theory is rarely rejected by a church built on the life, death, and resurrection of Jesus Christ. Jesus Christ was the ultimate example of servanthood by leaving all the glory of heaven to become a human and accepting the way of the cross. His earthly ministry built up a church that delivered the gospel to the ends of the earth after He ascended into heaven again. An example of his servant leadership is when Christ himself wraps a towel about Himself to wash His disciple's feet as His final lesson to them. This action certainly exemplifies servant leadership as a proper approach to leading others. He led by example, being that of a man of high stature, taking care of those who were under his care. Though in practice, servant leadership is as common in Christian organizations as it is in secular corporations.

While church leaders salute Jesus Christ as the model servant leader and affirm the servant leader approach loudly, in actual operation, many church leaders practice leadership as Gentiles did in real life.

But Jesus called them unto him, and said, Ye know that the princes of the Gentiles exercise dominion over them, and they that are great exercise authority upon them. But it shall not be so among you: but whosoever will be great among you, let him be your minister; And whosoever will be chief among you, let him be your servant: Even as the Son of man came not to be ministered unto, but to minister, and to give his life as a ransom for many. (Matthew 20:25-28)

Church leaders must value people, for they are God's handiwork. Listening to people is important in the church. This is how the Holy Spirit guides the church through its people, not just through the designated leader. Church leaders must be people developers more than program pushers. People development is the church's product. The church does not make a product; it is the product. Churches do not just have community events and parties to attract new people, but they do so to build up the community in which they are in, to become what the church is to be – a community of the saints. Community building is a primary task of the church leader and with adhering to the responsibilities of a leader, it is possible for the church to be the heart of its community.

ETHICAL MOTIVATIONS IN
THE LEADER

Church leaders must be authentic people who inspire trust. Talking about big dreams for the people to follow is not enough. People follow leaders, not dreams. They follow leaders who are trustworthy and have integrity; The leaders in the church must be men and women with a vision and the ability to plan for the future while also being able to determine and implement goals within the church. In the church, the vision is not to solely increase the size of the congregation but to put the vision into reality with the focus of mirroring God's kingdom. In being able to do so, a church leader must guide and support the members to see God's vision directly from God, not just from the church leaders and pastor.

Once the congregation itself has a concrete understanding of the vision and are in alignment with the pastor, the followers can then be trusted with decision making power on how their church can become what God desires. After all, the clergy do not get filled with a different Holy Ghost than the laity.

How the pastor leading the congregation exemplifies servant leadership, and it may be of concern for church leaders because part of their job is to motivate people to do the right thing.

Several popular theories of motivation are discussed in the leadership literature and are usually based on a psychological explanation that helps leaders and managers better understand their workers according to the Learned Needs Theory by David McClelland's in 1962 (Gordon). In his early work, he stated that many human needs are acquired from the culture, specifically the need for power (Gordon). When a need is strong, individuals will choose a behavior that meets that need. Such needs were developed from copying what one observes in their environment and tends to occur more often when behavior is rewarded more frequently. This theory also complements the views of situational leadership theory that may focus on task and/or relationship management.

In the X and Y Theory, Douglas McGregor believed that managers hold certain assumptions about people in the organizational settings. The theory X style of management arose from a fundamental attribution error in which managers assumed that an employee's lack of motivation was a disposition rather than a function of unmotivating work situations (Carraher, 2015). One can interpret a lack of motivation as people being lazy and requiring structure and direction. Without direction, they will act irresponsibly. In contrast, Theory Y relies heavily on self-control and self-direction (McGregor & Cutcher-Gershenfeld, 2008). This theory assumes that people are not lazy, do not have to be closely supervised, and want to work-- especially when the work is meaningful and challenging. Argyris and Schon (1982), argue that leaders need to take care that they do not treat others with Theory Y statements espoused theory and then behave with Theory X assumption theory in action.

Expectancy Theory Victor Vroom theory of motivation is a more complex theory.

Expectancy theory holds that the human behavior is a function of the perceived worth of rewards that certain behavior provides, and that the expectation of the performer will provide that reward (Quick, 1988). His theory assumes that most behavior is under the voluntary control of the person. Behavior is related to outcome and success; however, the value and attractiveness of these outcomes varies from one to another. Within the church, this could be represented by a church member having more motivation within the church knowing that their work will be rewarded with a position in the church such as a mother, secretary, deacon and more.

Positive Reinforcement by B.F. Skinner emphasized the external situation in his approach to personality and motivation. Skinner's positive reinforcement theory is one of the most used methods in which one's behavior is strengthened or increased based on consequences (Wei & Yazdanifard, 2014). The Skinnerian view is an extreme behaviorist approach and sees an individual as a passive victim of events in his or her environment. As a pastor, continued praise after a job well done or an offered reward of some sort, as well as increased responsibility can all aid in the change of behavior. In this way, the member is continually receiving a positive reward for doing God's work.

Most theories of motivation support the belief that leaders can influence the motivation state of others. When leaders take an active role in motivating others, they are being cognizant to the motivational needs, as well as seeking to implement and maintain structure so that everyone is aware of the vision that belongs to the church as a community member who is interested in the church.

Motivation is a concern for church leaders because part of their job is to motivate people to do the right thing. Churches are always seeking volunteers to work in the nursery, youth ministry, or to fulfill the Great Commission within the church. The motivation to increase volunteerism is aligned with Matthew 28:19-20, "Go ye therefore, and teach all nations, baptizing them in the name of the Father, and of the Son, and of the Holy Ghost, teaching them to observe all things whatsoever I have commanded you: and, lo, I am with you always, even unto the end of the world. Amen." (Bible source). We teach in hopes that one will follow and help other incoming members do the same. This allows for responsibility to be shared and lessens the load for the pastor. Sound member involvement is ideally the overall goal.

Pastors and church leaders must be motivators and realize that intrinsic motivation is more powerful and long-lasting than extrinsic motivation. However, there is theological reason why ministers should care, not just about whether the people are motivated, but also the why behind how they are motivated. In Christian thinking, the quality of a deed or service is not based on the deed itself but rather on the motivation. This notion is most prominent in the teaching of Jesus on the hypocrites praying publicly. Matthew 6:1-18-6 reads:

Take heed that ye do not offer your alms before men, to be seen of them: otherwise ye have no reward of your Father which is in heaven. Therefore when thou doest thine alms, do not sound a trumpet before thee, as the hypocrites do in the synagogues and in the streets, that they may have glory of men. Verily I say unto you, They have their reward. But when thou doest alms, let not thy left hand know what thy right hand doeth: That thine alms may be in secret: and thy Father which seeth in secret himself shall reward thee openly. And when thou Prayerst thou shalt not be as the hypocrites are: for they love to pray standing in the synagogues and in the corners of the streets, that they may be seen of men. Verily I say unto you, they have their reward. But thou, when thou prayest, enter into thy closet, and when thou hast shut thy door, pray to thy Father which is in secret; and thy Father which seeth in secret shall reward thee openly. But when ye pray, use not vain repetitions, as the heathen do: for they think that they shall be heard for their much speaking. Be not ye therefore like unto them: for your Father knoweth what things ye have need of, before ye ask him. After this manner therefore pray ye: Our Father which art in heaven, Hallowed be thy name. Thy kingdom come, Thy will be done in earth, as it is in heaven. Give us this day our daily bread And forgive us our debts, as we forgive our debtors. And lead us not into temptation, but deliver us from evil: For thine is the kingdom, and the power, and the glory, forever. Amen. For if ye forgive men their trespasses, your heavenly Father will also forgive you: But if ye forgive not men their trespasses, neither will your Father forgive your trespasses. Moreover when ye fast, be not, as the hypocrites, of a sad countenance: for they disfigure their faces, that they may appear unto men to fast. Verily I say unto you, they have their reward. But thou, when thou fastest, anoint thine head, and wash thy face; That thou appear not unto men to fast, but unto thy Father which is in secret: and thy Father, which seeth in secret, shall reward thee openly.

Christian leaders have a considerable amount of concern in people being motivated to do a right deed or service for the reward but also that their motive be for the right reasons. Therefore, theories of motivation are highly important for church leaders and implementing the best theory or a blend of theories for their specific congregation is key.

The implication of the theories previous discussed (Theory X and Y, Expectancy Theory, and Positive Reinforcement) is which one to use for yielding the best response from the members and/or volunteers in the church. Churches have always been aware of motivating people, but a leader who is conscious of how to motivate the congregation can be more effective at getting people to respond and stay in the church.

For example, people want to belong and be a part of a church. The membership and the ability to be connected to an organization is worthwhile for many because it gives them the ability to be part of and contribute to their community or the community that the church is located in. Not only do people want to be part of the community, for the most part, many yearn for the ability to participate and have a say in decision making within the church. The ability to vote and/or have authority in a certain department within the church is important to many. Nonetheless, the leader must decipher those who are genuine in their desire for a voice and input and those who are doing it just for a title. Through selecting the correct leadership style, the leader will be able to select the correct individual(s) and lead them in such a way to allow for full growth and a mirroring of the leadership standards of the pastor. In doing so, responsibility would be alleviated from the pastor, and members would see additional members following the vision of the church and the individual(s) in authority may become more respected in the church.

If this individual can properly exemplify the leadership role, they may acquire pride and become more invested in the church. This will allow for less turnover and increased dedication and longevity in members. One must remember that this all begins with the pastor determining the best leadership style and thoroughly implementing and supporting it until the members are vetted into the vision and the church.

Proverbs 21: 1-8 states:

Good leadership is a channel of water controlled by God; he directs it to whatever ends he chooses. We justify our actions by appearances; God examines our motives. Clean living before God and justice with our neighbors mean far more to God than religious performance. Arrogance and pride—distinguishing marks in the wicked—are just plain sin. Careful planning puts you ahead in the long run; hurry and scurry puts you further behind. Make it to the top by lying and cheating; get paid with smoke and a promotion—to death! The wicked get buried alive by their loot because they refuse to use it to help others. Mixed motives twist life into tangles; pure motives take you straight down the road.

It is also possible that an individual pastor or church leader might be inclined to motivate others using the motivator that he himself would be most motivated by. However, what the pastor must realize is that each member/volunteer is different and is motivated differently. Some people are motivated intrinsically, while other are motivated by extrinsic factors. The pastor must gain an understanding of how each potential leader likes to be motivated. He or she can do this by creating a questionnaire for a prospective leader to complete to gain an understanding of which leadership style to implement.

Recognizing which is the master motivator for an individual leader and reviewing an examination of what may not motivate them can help the leader develop a broader approach to the motivation of others. "Know yourself" is good advice when implementing a system to build leadership within the church with current members/volunteers.

Most leadership literature assumes a need for some form of power in the leader. Harvard social psychologist, David McClelland, found that effective leadership is motivated by a set of three learned motivations: affiliation, power, and achievement.

Kanungo and Mendonca applied these three motivations to build an ethical model for leaders. They suggested both positive and negative expressions for each of

McClelland's motivations. McClelland's three motivations and the Kanungo and Mendonca positive/negative expressions are explained in a manner of association with key details. (Kanungo & Mendonca, 1996). They are explained as follows: Affiliation is McClelland's first motivation, which is defined as a need for friendship and social contact. Kanungo and Mendoca stated that the negative expression of affiliation is avoidance for fear of rejection. In contrast, the positive expression is being approachable with a concern for others (Kanungo & Mendonca, 1996).

Achievement is McClelland's second motivation factor, which is defined as the need for production, responsibility, realizing goals, and solving problems. Kanungo and Mendoca explain the negative aspect of achievement as for having personal gain only and the positive aspect as acquiring social achievements or collective capability (Kanungo & Mendonca, 1996).

Lastly, the third type of motivation is power, which McClelland describes as the need for impact, authority, pressure, and winning arguments. Kanungo and Mendoca identifies the negative affect as being person, emphasizing dominance and submission, and self-aggrandizement. They then identify the positive effects as being institutional, persuasive, and inspirational for purposes of the organization (Kanungo & Mendonca, 1996).

Kanungo and Mendonca suggest that altruism is the value that drives the positive versus the negative expressions in each of the . above categories. The intent of altruism is to benefit others and the positive is the antidote to a negative motivation. Intent is to benefit self, as it moderates or overcomes the effect of the negative option for each intrinsic motivation.

The authors observed organizational leaders as being consistently effective only when they were motivated by concern for others, even when it resulted in some cost of self. The author proposes the following: for a leader to achieve an altruistic vision for their organization and the people in it, they must first assess the environment. Instead of focusing on their own inward needs and omitting the follower's needs, the leader must shift their paradigm and focus on the welfare of the whole organization, while keeping in mind the vision.

Earlier we discussed creating and implementing a vision to then lead the members/volunteers of the church into following or abiding by that vision. Here we discuss the vision and being willing to assume the risk of seeing the potential in all followers and articulating the vision in a way they can understand.

Secondly, one must implement the plan. Through encouragement, empowerment, shared decision making, and modeling, people can grow into effective leaders. According to McClelland, motivations are not fixed on attributes but can be learned, unlearned, and changed. He believes that the formation of a positive motivation happens only as the leader matures through developmental stages.

Leadership is more than a position. It is a moral relationship between people held together by loyalty and trust, rooted in the leader's commitment to values and accountability when exercising their power and authority. This requires leaders to be ethical and consistent in their championed values and behavior.

For church leaders, the motivation should be and is as important as the result. William Law and John Wesley believe right intentions are even more important than right actions. The Pharisees of Jesus' day were condemned by Jesus not for their wrong actions of praying or fasting but for their wrong motivations to be seen and praised by others, which is exemplified in Matthew 6.

The church leader can say, "Well, it worked, and we grew, so it is good." In defending that position, the ends justify the means. A leader might say, "The motivation is as important as the result." The motivation is your vision and purpose; with a strong vision and perhaps with one's followers, the desired result is bound to take place.

Research on ethical motivations help church leaders face and ponder their own motivation for leading the church. With the several different intrinsic and extrinsic motivations previous discussed, a church leader picks or blends a theory or multiple theories with the vision of the church and places an understanding of their members in the forefront.

When a church leader has determined the theory or theories that they prefer to mimic, they can then ask themselves the questions: "Why do you want to succeed" or "What are your motives to do better?" These two questions are similar to the questions that a CEO may ask themselves in regard to their company.

One can observe the similarities of a pastor leading his congregation and that of a CEO leading his or her company. Previously discussed, within businesses in the United States there are three primary types of motivations. These motivations include being a part of a great group of people, having affiliation, and to accomplish something great or to make a real impact in life by having power.

When church members feel aligned to the vision of the church, agree with how the pastor is leading the church, and are active members, they can experience those three different types of motivations and take pride in their church. This then allows for ease of the volunteers/members fulfilling the vision of the church, taking on responsibility to lessen the load of the pastor, and helping guide new members in fulfilling the vision of the church as well with positive intentions.

Along with the church members, the church leader can also use the three described motivations as factors in what attracts them to leadership in the church. Each of the three motivations have both a positive and negative manifestation. Church leaders should put aside relationship avoidance or excessive clinging relationships for negative affiliation. They should resist temptation to work only for personal gain and career development for negative achievement. They should reject the impulse to build a personal kingdom of power. Rather, a Christian church leader should steer their motivations toward the positive side of these three. Building strong social groups with positive affiliation, working for the collective achievements of the local church, and building the institution of the church and kingdom of God are key.

DECISION MAKING

V room and Yetton proposed a series of procedures for making decisions, ranging from unilateral directive by the leader without input, to highly participatory forms of decision making (Vroom & Yetton, 2017). Their procedures were an early decision flow process model designed to help a leader determine whether directive or participative decision making would be more appropriate. This deduction approach to decision making assumes that no one style is best for all situations. The choice of style depends on whether the leader is aiming for decision quality, subordinate's acceptance of the decision, or some combination of these (Vroom & Yetton, 2017). The Vroom and Yetton model has six decision procedures. The procedures are grouped into three different categories: autocratic, consultative and group based. Within each procedure there are two different types.

The first procedural is autocratic. Within this procedure, the first type includes a focus on decision making. The leader solves the problem with the information they have. The second type is to collect information and decide. The leader collects information from subordinates and then uses that information to make an informed decision (Vroom & Yetton, 2017).

The second procedure is consultation decision making. Within this procedure, first type, the leader shares the problem individually, collects ideas, and makes a sound decision. The leader shares the problem individually with followers, gathers suggestions, and then makes the decision. For the second type, the leader also shares the problem with the group, collects ideas, and makes a decision. The leader shares the problem with subordinates as a group, reflecting their collective ideas and then uses that information to make a decision (Vroom & Yetton, 2017).

The third procedure is group participative decision making. For the first type, the leader initially shares the problem individually, collects alternative solutions, and makes a consensus decision. The leader shares the problem individually, generates alternative solutions, and attempts to reach consensus on a decision. For the second type withing this procedure, the leader shares problems with the group, develops alternative solutions and makes a consensus decision. The leader shares the problem guiding the group to generate alternative solutions, attempting to reach consensus as a group on a decision (Vroom & Yetton, 2017).

A year later, Vroom and Jago added a seventh choice to the above list, which is delegated decision making. This procedure consists of the leader delegating the entire problem to a subordinate and giving responsibility and support for his or her solution (Vroom & Jago, 1988).

These procedures allow awareness of different leadership types. Vroom and Yetton developed a yes/no questionnaire assisting in determining what decision style to use by eliminating one or more of the options from the directive or participative continuum above. The questionnaire includes seven questions to help diagnose the demands of the situation.

For reference, the questions asked in the questionnaire are as follows (Vroom & Yetton, 2017):

1. Does the problem possess a quality requirement?

2. Does the leader have sufficient information to make a high-quality decision?

3. Is the problem structured?

4. Are acceptances of the decision by subordinates important for effective implementation?

5. If the leader were to make the decision alone, are they reasonably certain that it would be accepted by subordinates?

6. Do subordinates share the organizational goals to be attained in solving this problem?

7. Is conflict among subordinates likely in preferred solutions?

After an individual has completed the questionnaire, they then have some guidance on the best motivation procedure and the type to proceed with.

Decision making in the church is not just a matter of who has the power and what would be the best thing to do is. Instead, decisions made have theological implications and they are coupled with motivational theories that one may use in a business. One must be driven by the Word but also be cognizant of the members and the importance of their followship. In doing so, a motivation theory is then applied to help the volunteers/members follow the leadership of the church leader. As described earlier, these members help with the delegation of responsibilities in the church, leading others towards the vision of the church, and overall allow the church leader to spend less time on minuscule acts or activities.

For example, I am currently deciding if the church should stay downtown in Puyallup, Washington within the present facility and continue to minister to the current neighborhood or move out to the suburbs to minister in an area with new housing developments. With this major decision, I am trying to base my decision on theologically principals. This decision calls more for a consultative decision-making procedure discussed earlier. As the leader, I would not independently make the decision to change locations, but I would consult my board and possibly some of the members.

I then have to ask myself the question of, "What is God's will?" Some churches may assume there is no such thing as God's will in their decisions, at least the important ones. But that is not correct, being that we are based on God's will. Seeking God's will be part of the process in Christian decision making.

The point is, the decision-making power is a theological matter to the church, followed by the church leader maintaining their theology integrity as they manage the decision-making process. Some of the implications of Vroom and Yetton's decision-making models for church leaders may be:

Few pastors can run their church as if they were the owner or manager. Therefore, a pastor usually must become a master at managing the decision-making process not the master decision maker.

Pastors should avoid manipulation of the decision-making process. Local church decision-making power is often given to the trustee board, yet the pastor is the trained professional leader and often knows which is the best solution. Therefore, a challenging situation often develops in church leadership. The pastor knows the best solution but does not have the power to decide. In these situations, the pastor may set up a process that looks very much like the participatory decision-making process, but it is a process where the pastor can manipulate the church board into deciding what the pastor has already pre-determined is the right decision. If all goes smoothly, nobody will notice. But if the hidden solutions of the pastor receive resistance, the pastor's manipulation of the process often becomes more evident, and the laity feels manipulated. How does a pastor avoid this predicament? Usually, a pastor can bring laity into the decision-making process at the consultative level even before the pastor has determined what the decision should be. While manipulative leadership can make things happen for a time, eventually it will erode the pastor's credibility as a leader and ultimately become counterproductive.

In large churches, the pastor may use this process more with staff than the board. However, the decision-making process in a larger mega church is different than that of an average size church. No matter what the population, decision-making power in large churches often gravitate to the full-time paid staff. What was once done by the board or committees is now done by the professional staff. In these churches, sometimes the board becomes more like a College Board of Trustees, dealing mostly with financial issues and replacing the senior pastor when they resign or need to leave for other reasons. In larger churches the decision-making process outlined above often reflects the senior pastor's role with staff ministers, and therefore this process has more in common with the business process from which these models emerged. A senior pastor, for example, should determine which of the seven procedures will work best for decisions to be made about staff specialties, such as youth camp, the Easter program, or Sunday school classes.

CONFLICTS

C onflict occurs in all segments of organizations. The question is not the existence of conflict but how to manage it. What is the character, intensity, and manner in which the conflict is expressed or channeled? When handling conflict, one can be a positive or negative force, but it is all determined by how you manage the conflict. Some do not know how to handle conflict and need to be taught or have it modeled for them. It is part of the leader's responsibility to model how to handle conflict and its related issues of power, values, and changes constructively. If it is not modeled or handled, you run the risk of jeopardizing the church because a solution has not been proposed or implemented. Many leaders see conflict as an opportunity to develop their followers.

Morton Deutsch found that conflict between parties that had a cooperative relationship rather than a competitive relationship were likely to be less destructive (Deutsch, 1973). Destructive conflict has a tendency to escalate and expand beyond the initial cause. Therefore, it is important for leaders to continually strengthen an environment of conflict-limiting factors, such as encouragement of creative thinking, commitment to cooperation, and "benevolent misperception" minimizing differences and enhancing flaws (Deutsch, 1973). Each attribute allows conflict to be taken care of within boundaries. Leaders must avoid negative competition and power tactics, lack of communication, and over sensitivity within the environment because he can negatively impact conflict, even if it is to cultivate positivity in the end. Deutsch states that the truth of "cooperation breeds cooperation, while competitions breed competition" and this statement has many applications for leaders of organizations (Deutsch, 1973).

Communication expert, Gerald Goldhaber, who wrote Organizational Communication, believes group conflict, which can be within or between groups and tear apart or decrease its activity, may actually tend to bring members together and increase their activity (Goldhaber, 1990).

Goldhaber recommends allowing time for each side to describe their own image and the perception of the other's view, followed by reporting the perspective to their other group. After they have done so, separate discussions of what may cause the discrepancy in the varying perceptions on the issues occur. Finally, the groups come together to suggest their alternative solutions and compromises for the problem (Goldhaber, 1990). This process will allow leaders to encourage planning on how to relate differently toward each other in the future.

Ken Sande is another author who has published work regarding conflict. He addressed personal conflict resolution from his experience as a lawyer and as a Christian. He believed that lawsuits tend to drive people further apart and there should be a better way. Peacemaker Ministries began in 1982 for resolving conflicts out of the court in a cooperative manner, rather than through an adversarial manner in the legal system. In order to help people change the attitudes and habits that led to the conflict, he leads the involved parties through four basic stages (Sande & Johnson, 2008):

1. Glorify God. (I Corinthians 10:31 Whether therefore ye eat, or drink, or whatsoever ye do, do all to the glory of God). Showing

a complete love for God protects from impulsive, self-centered behaviors that escalate conflict (Sande & Johnson, 2008).

2. Get the log out of your eye. (Matthew 7:5 Thou hypocrite, first cast out the beam out of thine own eye, and then shalt thou see clearly to cast out the mote out of thy brother's eye). One must face up to their own attitudes, faults, and responsibilities before pointing out what others did wrong (Sande & Johnson, 2008).

3. Go and show your brother his fault. (Matthew 18:15 Moreover if thy brother shall trespass against thee, go and tell him about his fault between thee and him alone: if he shall hear thee, thou hast gain thy brother). Confronting constructively when others fail to accept responsibility for their actions may require other neutral individuals to help restore peace (Sande & Johnson, 2008).

4. Go and be reconciled (Matthew 5:24 Leave there thy gift to the altar, and there rememberest that thy brother, and then come and offer thy gift). Committing to restoring damaged relationships requires forgiveness and cooperative negotiation (Sande & Johnson, 2008).

Sande believes God's peacemaking principles may be applied in the home, workplace, church, and neighborhood. He expands on each with helpful questions for the leader to guide the parties through the process of conflict resolution.

Jesus was the great peacemaker. In one of the Beatitudes, He bless peacemakers, yet elsewhere Jesus also said He did not come to bring peace but a sword. Both Jesus and Paul offer specific instructions on handling conflict between believers in the church. The church, while reflecting a perfect body in Heaven, is essentially an earthly institution.

As an earthly institution including less than perfect human beings with varied experiences, opinions and representing varied cultures, we can expect conflict in the church and among denominations. However, conflict in the church does not always derive from our human tendencies but can also be prompted by supernatural influences. Division, strife, and sectarianism (i.e., being of Paul vs. Apollos) are sometimes condemned in scripture as more than human frailties, but by sin and prompting by the Devil. Either way, church leaders will face conflict.

Experienced church leaders do not debate the existence of conflict so much as they try to determine how to avoid, resolve, or mange them. Some of the implications of conflict resolution theory for church leaders may be that every church leader must decide their view on conflict. We can then ask the following questions: "Is conflict in the church something bad that should be avoided?" "Is conflict bad, but should be expected and resolved?" "Is conflict a good sign of health and diversity and should be managed by the church leader?"

Many church leaders have not determined their theological stance on conflict in the church. Most church leaders need more thought on their ecclesiology to determine where conflict fits in their view of the church. Once this decision is made, the church leader can approach conflict to resolve it or to manage it.

Goldhaber raises the question for church leaders as to the potential good results of conflict. Is there more conflict in a church that is changing, growing, and doing new things than a church that is static, declining, or predictable? To what extent is conflict between denominations or local churches a good thing? How can a leader manage conflict in a way that produces greater gains for the kingdom?

Ken Sande and Peacemaker Ministries provide a summary of the biblical approach to conflict management and resolution. This appears to be a formula presented by Jesus two thousand years ago that all churches and individuals can use today. What would a church look like that implemented this practice? How would a church implement the four steps previously described to maintain and apply as practice within the local body?

A conflict that I have experienced within the church is a senior pastor, who as the church leader, insists that the people go to the offending party (soloist, Sunday school teacher, youth pastor) and address their concerns with them directly, instead of involving a third party to mediate. Though does this alleviate responsibility from the church because no one is serving as a mediator? Does this help with conflict with the church in a positive manner because individuals are addressing issues immediately with one another? Or is a mediator needed, and if not the church leader, a designated trusted leader within the church?

In this instance, guidance, leadership, modeling and teaching how to positively resolve conflict and communicate with one another would allow the previous described situation to occur in a more positive manner than in a negative manner. However, if the participating parties do not have the conflict-resolution skills, it is best to have a mediator. If the church leader desires to lessen his or her responsibility, then it is their duty to designate and train others to mediate without a bias conflict among members.

Certainly, the most effective church leaders learn the skill of practicing conflict limiting practices, including high levels of cooperation instead of competition and power tactics, with a heavy emphasis on communication, creative thinking, and developing a culture of what

Deutsch calls "benevolent misperception" (grace) to keep the environment from becoming destructive.

According to Dr. John Maxwell, leaders resolving conflict by confrontation is difficult; two things have to happen for us to become better leaders and both deal with confrontation. We must settle for the person or the group. We must do so in the spirit of love, and both of these things have to happen. If a leader does not confront, they will never settle the major issues and they will never be the leader God wants them to be and will also be operating on less than their potential. If we do not confront in love, those who work for us under those circumstances will struggle (Maxwell, 2019).

Before a leader confronts anyone about a problem or situation, they must make sure it is not a problem they face in their own personal life. "Is this an issue I need to deal with myself?" is the first question a leader should ask themselves. It does not do any good spiritually to confront someone else about a problem that is affecting you in their own life. Leaders resolve conflicts, but sometimes it could be your own personal problem that influences you to confront the other person. This situation is aligning with Luke 6:41-42 which reads:

And why beholdest thou the mote that is in thy brother's eye, but perceives not the beam that is in thine own eye? Either how canst thou say to thy brother, Brother, let me pull out the mote that is in thine eye, when thou thyself beholdest not the beam that is in thine own eye? Thou hypocrite, cast out first the beam out of thine own eye, and then shalt thou see clearly to pull out the mote that is in thy brother's eye. (King James Version, 1989)

CONFLICT RESOLUTION

C onflicts are unavoidable just like motion causes friction. If we as individuals are moving and involved in different actions and communications, the friction or conflict is inevitable because we all have our own ideas and theories. If you lead people, then you must realize that you are going to deal with conflict. As pastors and church leaders our jobs consist of dealing with people. Confrontation will be something we will never completely eliminate leading people and as an organization.

One must realize that when you are dealing with people in motion, friction will come. The more people you have, the more friction you deal with. If you can settle issues and problems in your own life, confrontation will become easier for you because you will come to realize that this is a part of your job. According to Dr. John Maxwell, "People tend to avoid conflict due to fear." According to Joy Life Ministry, there are six reasons why it is difficult to confront fear:

1. There is a fear of being disliked; Nobody wants to be disliked, we want everybody to love us. Every time you must confront someone, you risk them disliking you.

2. There is a fear of rejection; We may be afraid that people will reject what we say. They may even leave the organization and

spread the wrong information about us, withhold their tithes, offering, etc.

3. There is a fear of creating anger or a fear of making things worse; I do not believe that confrontation makes matters worse; however, I do believe what can make a situation worse is the spirit of confrontation. If you have a bad attitude, and do not control your emotions, it can only make matters worse.

4. Phariseeism; Sometimes it is difficult to confront people about certain problems and issues because we know that these very issues are problems in our own lives that we have not dealt with. You say to yourself. "How can I confront that person about this situation when I know I have the same problem in my life?"

5. Sharing our feelings; A lot of confrontation is intuitive and expresses how we feel.

6. Lack of skill to be able to cope with and/or manage confrontation; Sometimes the reason we do not confront others is because we have not been taught confrontation skills. The leader should never take the "winner takes all" attitude. Leaders must be open minded and never say that there will be no compromise, which should never be your attitude in any confrontation. I have learned at several seminars various ways handle conflicts.

Many people walk away from conflict; they believe that it is easier to avoid it than to tackle. This may be due to the unknown, such as the unknown of not knowing how the other party or parties will respond to addressing the conflict. We want to keep the peace at all costs. I am not saying that there are right and wrong choices. Before I get in a difficult personal situation, first I ask myself, "Am I holding back for my personal comfort or for the good of the organization?" and "Am I doing what makes me comfortable?"

If I do what is good for the organization and it happens to make me feel comfortable, I must remember that two wrongs do not make a right. There are times when we should walk away from conflict, but there are times we must confront conflict.

Sometimes we must stick our heads in the sand and say, "It will go away." Surprisingly, many times this is the best option to consider. Leaders can diffuse minor incidents to the status of significant problems simply by agreeing to discuss the matter further. The insightful leader needs to be aware of how to manage and address different types of conflicts and be cognizant of the personalities and spiritual walk of the parties that are experiencing differences that need to be confronted. Since most leaders are not looking for additional work, this option to confront independently can be useful; but members need to be trained to do so.

As believers, we should be concerned in a positive sense about others. Notice the following scriptures:

1. Philippians 2:4, "Look not every man on his own things, but ever man also on the things of others."

2. Matthew 5:23-24, "Therefore if thou bring thy gift to the altar, and there remembers that thy brother hath out against thee. Leave there thy gift before the altar, and go thy way, first be reconciled to thy brother, and then come and offer thy gift."

3. Hebrews 10:24, "And let us consider one another to provoke unto love and to good works."

4. Galatians 6:1, "Brethren, if a man be overtaken in a fault, ye which are spiritual, restore such a one on the spirit of meekness, considering thyself, lest thou also be tempted."

5. Ephesians 4:14, "That we henceforth be no more children, tossed to and from, and carried about with every wind of doctrine, by the sleight of men, and cunning craftiness, whereby they lie in wait to deceive. But speaking the truth in love may grow up into him in all things, which is the head, even Christ."

When you must deal or manage confrontation, it is best to keep the above scriptures in mind to help guide you through the situation. To get a better understanding you must know what is on the individual's mind.

In my preparation to reason with a man, I spent one-third of my time thinking about myself and what I should say and two-thirds thinking about him and what he is going to say.

As Christians, we confront not to embarrass, belittle, tear down, or humiliate; we confront because of our commitment to help others reach their potential, including a full-fledged stature in Christ.

Notice what Paul says in Colossians 1:10, "That ye might walk worthy of the Lord unto all pleasing, being fruitful in every good work, and increasing in the knowledge of God."

We must always confront with the right spirit. According to Romans 1:10, "Making request, if any means now at length I might have a prosperous journey by the will of God."

Being a leader, we are committed to the Lord and His goals for us. Therefore, it is part of our job to help our brothers and sisters to mature in Christ with the right spirit. Galatians 6:1 states, "Brethren, if a man be overtaken in a fault, ye which are spiritual, restore such a one in the spirt of meekness, considering thyself, lest thou be tempted." The above is also aligned with 2 Corinthians 10:1, "Now I, Paul, myself beseech you by meekness and gentleness of Christ, who in presence am based among you, but being absent am bold toward you."

Always start on a positive note. Be cautious when people say they agree with you in principle. This usually means they are getting ready to argue. Learn to structure what you need in this order by asking yourself the following questions: How would you describe what the other person is doing to cause a problem?" and "Are you always talking about me?" The "how" tells how this makes you feel and the "why" tells why this is important to you.

For example, if something causes you to cry or to become angry, always allow the person who is being confronted an opportunity to respond. They will not be ready to listen to reason until they have expressed their emotions or had time to swallow the hurt. Repeat or rephrase the person's explanation. This will help the confronted person understand you know their position. Allow them to explain why they feel the confrontation was right or wrong. Indicate the desired action to be taken. Going through this process allows the focus to be on the future. The person who wants to change will gravitate toward possibly making things better. Reiterate the positive strengths of the person. What gets rewarded gets done. Put the issues in the past. Never bring it up again unless the problem reoccurs, or you use it to affirm positive change and growth.

Salvage a Confrontation Ambush

Nothing takes God by surprise. God is omniscient; He knows everything, and if He allows it, there is a reason, and I can choose to benefit from it. Ask God for wisdom and ask for others' opinions. James 1:5 states, "If any of you lack wisdom, let him ask God, that giveth to all men liberally, and upbraided not, and is shall be given him."

Separate the message from the messenger. It is difficult, but the message is more important because of what is said and not who is saying it. Do not become emotionally involved. Do not be defensive. If you are having difficulty, please reference the following scriptures:

1. Proverbs 1:15, "My son, walk not thou in the way with them, refrain thy foot from their path."

2. Proverbs 12:1, "Whoso loveth instruction loveth knowledge: but he that hateth reproof is brutish."

3. Proverbs 12:15, "The way of a fool is right in his own eyes: but he that heartened unto counsel."

4. Proverbs 12:25, "Heaviness in the heart of man maketh it stops, but a good word maketh it glad."

5. Proverbs 23:12, "Apply thine heart unto instruction, and thine ears to the words of knowledge."

6. Proverbs 12:12, "The wicked desireth the net of evil men: but the root of the righteous yielded fruit."

7. Proverbs 28:13, "He that covereth his sins shall not prosper: but whoso confesseth and forsake them shall have mercy."

Work in areas of truth. J Oswald Sanders states in his book *Spiritual Leadership,* "Every call for help is by no means necessarily a call from God. For every such call cannot be responded to. If the Christian leader sincerely plans his day in the Lord's presence and carries out that plan to the best of his ability (that is all that God requires), he then must leave it there. His responsibilities extend only to the matter or plan that lies within his control, the rest he can truthfully commit to his loving and competent Heavenly Father (Sanders, 2017)."

All leaders should seek reconciliation. In Romans 12:18 it states, "If it be possible, as much as Lieth in you live peaceably with all men."

Ecclesiastes, 4:9-12 can also be used for reference. "Two are better than one, because they have a good reward for their labor. For if they fall, the one will lift up his fellow: but woe to him that is alone when he Falleth for he hath not another to help up. And if one prevail against him, two shall withstand him, and a threefold cord is not quickly broken."

In the book *Inside Out* by Larry Crabb, it reads, "Between the time when God gave us life, and the time when he provided all the joys of this life, he intended to change us into people who can more deeply enjoy him now and represent him well to others" (Crabb,

2013). The urgency required to make that change is always painful, but God will settle for nothing less than deep changes in our character by transformation and restructuring how we approach life. If leaders are willing to learn and implement these principles of biblical confrontation, it will lighten their load when they must confront an individual or a group in their organization.

THE MAKING OF A GOOD LEADER

P astor Rick Warner did a seminar titled "What It Takes to be a Good Leader" (2013). He focused on eight biblical character- istics that would help develop good leadership skills when applied with the right spirit at the right time. These leadership principles are found in the book of Nehemiah.

The foundation of leadership is character not charisma. Character consists of the disposition, natural personality, and the distinctive quality of a person or thing. Charisma consists of the feature, tech- nicality, difference, or any part of the facial expression that portrays as the main attraction. The following are eight characteristics given in the book of Nehemiah, and if they are administered in the proper manner and at the proper time, you will have a portion of what it takes to be good leader.

The first characteristic is compassion; sympathy and tenderness. Nehemiah 1:4 reads "And it came to pass, when I heard these words, that I set down and wept and mourned certain days, and fasted, and prayed before God of heaven." Nehemiah wept and mourned over Jerusalem when he heard that the wall and graves of his ancestors were destroyed.

Compassion also describes a person's feelings and of putting themselves in someone's shoes so that they may be able to feel what he or she feels at the time of their suffering. Nehemiah has compassion for his people when he heard the bad news. Nehemiah 5:2-7: 2 reads:

> For there were that said, we, our sons, and our daughters, are many: therefore, we take up corn for them, that we may eat and live. Some also there were that said, we have mortgaged our lands, vineyards, and houses that we might buy corn for them, because of the dearth. There were also that said, we have borrowed money for the kin's tribute, and that upon our lands and vineyards. Yet now our flesh is as the flesh of our brethren, our children as their children, and lo, we bring into bondage our sons and our daughters to be servants, and some of our daughters are brought into bondage already, neither is it in our power to redeem them, for other men have our lands and vineyards. And I was very angry when I heard their cry and theses words. Then I consulted with myself, and I rebuked the nobles, and the rulers, and said unto them, ye exact usury, every one of his brothers, and set a great assembly against them.

Nehemiah reacted to the injustice that was administered to the poor. In verse six, "He was angry, he rebuked the nobles and the rulers for their mistreatment of the poor." He had compassion for the people, which is one of the characteristics of a good leader.

The second characteristic is contemplation: consider, meditate, reflect, view, purpose, and to propose. Nehemiah spent much time in prayer and meditation reflecting and thinking things through. Nehemiah 2:11-13: 11 reads,

So I came to Jerusalem and was there three days. And
I arose in the night, I and some few men with me,
neither told I, any man what my God had put in my
heart to do at Jerusalem. Neither was there any beast
with me, save the beast that I rode upon. And I went
out by night by the gate of the valley, even before the
dragon well, and to the dung port, and viewed the
walls of Jerusalem, which were broken down, and the
gates thereof were consumed with fire.

Nehemiah took a midnight ride around the city. He always took
the time to think before speaking. Referring back to Nehemiah 5:7,
"Then I consulted with myself, and I rebuked the nobles, and the
rulers and said unto them, yet exact usury, every one of his brothers,
and I set a great assembly against them." Nehemiah made his plans
to think it through, and he thought it through. (Other scripture references: Nehemiah 1:4-11, 2:4; 4:4-5,9;5:19;6:9, and 13:14,22).

The third characteristic is consideration: A point of importance, a
thing worth considering, thinks about the advantages and disadvan-
tages, to assess before reaching a decision. Nehemiah maintained a
positive attitude. He had never been sad before the king. Nehemiah
2:1; "And it came to pass in the month Nisan, in the twentieth year
of Artaxerxes that wine was before him: and I took up the wine and
gave it unto the king. Now I had not been before this time sad in his
presence."

God was the source of Nehemiah's strength. Nehemiah had great
concentration and always focused on his goals. He was a godly leader
in government – a man of wisdom, principle, courage, impeccable
integrity, unwavering faith, compassion for the oppressed, and gifted

in leadership and organizational skills. Nehemiah was a problem solver as illustrated in Chapter 2:7-8; 7,

Moreover, I said unto the king, if it please the king, let letters be given me to the governors beyond the river, that they may convey me over till I come to Judah…And a letter unto Asaph the keeper of the king's forest, that he may give me timber to make beams for the gates of the palace which appertained to the house, and for the wall of the city, and the house that I shall enter into, and the king granted me, according to the wall of the city, and for the house that I shall enter into, and the king granted me, according to the good hand of my God upon me. (King James Version, 1989)

Clearly, Nehemiah anticipated problems, yet remained focused. Every godly leader must learn how to stay focused on the project that God has assigned to him. When Sanballat heard that Nehemiah had the children of Israel rebuilding the wall, he became angry and mocked the Israelites saying, "What do these feeble Jews think? Do they think they can revive the stones out of the rubbish which are burned?" Then Tobiah the Ammonite was by him, and he said, "Even that which they build if a fox goes up he shall even break down their stone wall," Nehemiah 4:1-3. They continue to make threats against Nehemiah, but Nehemiah stayed focused on the project. He never left the work to meet with them. He assigned each father and son to set watch over their individual families. He posted them by families. Notice Nehemiah 4:13, "Therefore set I in the lower places behind the wall, and on the higher places, I even set the people after families with their swords, their spears, and their bows." He then created work shifts.

In addition, according to Nehemiah 4:16-18: 16:

And it came to pass from that time forth, that the half of my servants wrought in the work, and the other half of them held both the spears, the shields, and the bows, and the habergeons, and the rulers were behind all the house of Judah. They which builded on the wall, and they that bare burdens, with those that laded, everyone with one of his hands wrought in the work, and with his other hand held a weapon. For the builders, everyone had his sword girded by his side, and so builded. And he sounded the trumpet was by me.

The fourth characteristic is courage: bravery, valor, boldness, strength, enduring, heroism, defiance, strong-minded and keeping your chin up. A good leader can design strategies that produce resources. Nehemiah's creativity kept the enemies from invading the children of Israel while they were working on the walls. Nehemiah also showed courage when he asked the king for twelve years leave of absence. Nehemiah 2:5-6: 5 reads:

And I said unto the king, if it pleases the king, and if thy servant have found favor in thy sight, that thou wouldest send me unto Judah, unto the city of my father's sepulchers, that I may build it. And the king said unto me (the queen also sitting by him) for how long shall thy journey be? And when wilt thou return? So, it please the king to send me, and I set him a time.

As well, Nehemiah 5:14 reads:

Moreover from the time that I was appointed to be their governor in the land of Judah, from the twentieth year even unto the two and thirtieth year of Anaxerxes the king, that is twelve years, I and my brethren have not eaten the bread of the governor." Nehemiah showed courage when he responded to the enemy attacks. Notice Nehemiah 4:14; "And I looked, and rose up, and said unto the nobles, and to the rulers, and to the rest of the people. Be not ye afraid of them, remember the Lord, which is great and terrible, and fight for your brethren, your sons, and your daughters, your wives and your houses."

It is also supported in Nehemiah 5:7-13:

Then I consulted with myself, and I rebuked the nobles, and the rulers, and said unto them, Ye exact usury, every one of his brothers. And I set a great assembly against them. And I said unto them, we after our ability have redeemed our brethren the Jews, which were sold unto the heathen, and will ye even sell your brethren? Or shall they be sold unto us? Then held they their peace and found nothing to answer. Also, I said, it is not good that ye do: ought ye not to walk in the fear of our God because of the heathen our enemies? I likewise, and my brethren, and my servants, might exact of them money and corn, I pray you let us leave off this usury. Restore, I pray you, to them, even this day, their day, their lamb, their vineyards, their olive yards, and their houses, also the hundredth part of the money, and of the corn, the wine, and the oil, that ye exact of them. Then said they, we will restore them, and will require nothing of them, so will we do as thou sayest. Then I called the priests, and took an oath of them, that they should do according to this promise. Also I shook my lap, and said, So God shake out every man from his house, and from his labor that performeth not this promise, even thus be he shaken out, and emptied, And the entire congregation said, Amen, and praised the Lord. And the people did according to this promise."

Courage is not the absence of fear; it is moving ahead in spite of your fear. Nehemiah was a man of integrity, wholesomeness, oneness, and righteousness. Nehemiah had a clear conscience in business. He did not abuse his position, power, or privilege as a leader, even though he could have.

Notice also Nehemiah 5:14-19:

More over from the time that I was appointed to be their governor in the land of Judah, from the twentieth year even unto the two and thirtieth year of Artaxerxes the king, that is, twelve years, I and my brethren have not eaten the bread of the governor.15; But the former governors that had been before me were chargeable unto the people, and had taken of them bread and wine, beside forty shekels of silver, yea their servants bare rule over the people, but so did not I, because of the fear of God. 16; Yea, also I continued in the work of this wall, neither bought we any land: and all my servants were gathered thither unto the work. 17; Moreover, there were at my table a hundred and fifty of the Jews and rulers, beside those that came unto us from among the heathen that are about us. 18; Now that which was prepared for me daily was one ox and six choice sheep. Also fowls were prepared for me, and once in ten days store of all sorts of wine: yet for all this required not I the bread of the governor, because the bondage was heavy upon this people.19; Think upon me, my God, for good, according to all that I have done for this people. (King James Version, 1989)

Nehemiah always uses good judgment of right and wrong. He was sensible. He had a good understanding. He was aware of what was going on, and he was still able to reason and make good judgment. To be a good leader you must have a clear conscience.

The fifth characteristic is conviction: Strong belief. For he that cometh to God must believe that he is and that he is a rewarded of them that diligently seek him. Faith means that we believe God to be absolutely trustworthy. For the Psalmist in Psalms 121:3-5 put it this way. 3; "He will not suffer thy foot to be moved: He that keepeth thee will not slumber." 4; "Behold, he that keepeth Israel shall neither slumber nor sleep." 5; "The Lord is thy keeper: the Lord is thy shade upon thy right hand."

The lifestyle of a leader will either make him or break him. If he neglects the cultivation of humility and faith, he is in big trouble. On the other hand, if anyone sets himself to be God's kind of man, by God's grace, you can be the man God wants you to be. 2 Chronicles 16:9 reads, "For the eyes of the Lord run to and fro throughout the whole earth, to show himself strong on the behalf of them whose heart is perfect toward him. Herein thou hast done foolishly: therefore, from henceforth thou shalt have wars."

The Spiritual Lifestyle
of a Leader

The primary characteristic exhibited by leaders should be purity of life. Daniel 1:8 tells us, "But Daniel purposed in his heart that he would not defile himself with the portion of the king's meat, nor with wine which he drank: therefore, he requested of the prince of the eunuchs that he might not defile himself."

The apostle continued Christ's way of life. In 2 Corinthians 6:14-15 it reads:

> Be ye not unequally yoke together with unbelievers, for what fellowship hath righteous with unrighteousness? And what communion hath light with darkness? And what concord hath Christ with Belial? Or what part hath he that believeth with an infidel? And what agreement hath the temple of God with idols? For ye are the temple of the living God; as God hath said, I will dwell in them, and walk in them, and I will be their God, and they shall be my people.

Paul used the five questions just quoted to draw a line of boundaries between God and the opposition. On the other side, he lists lawlessness, darkness, Satan, unbelief, and false worship. He states that you cannot mix these two lists. A leader must choose to live on one side or the other. Leroy Elms states in his book, *Be the Leader You were Meant to be,* "The leader must set an example in his behavior according to the standards of the scriptures. Paul says in I Timothy 3:2; "A bishop then must be blameless, the husband of one wife, vigilant, sober, of good behavior, given to hospitality, apt to teach." I Samuel 16:7 reads; "But the Lord said unto Samuel, look not on his countenance, or on the height of his stature, because I have refused him: for the Lord seeth not as man seeth: for man looketh on the outward appearance, but the Lord looketh on the heart."

2 Timothy 2:19-21 reads:

Nevertheless the foundation of God standeth sure, having this seal. The Lord knoweth them that are his. And, let everyone that nameth the name of Christ depart from iniquity. But in a great house there are not only vessels of gold and some silver, but also of wood and of earth, and some honor, and some to dishonor. If a man therefore purge himself from these, he shall be vessel unto honor, sanctified, and meet for the master's use and prepared unto every good work.

The simple spiritual truth is that a man can choose which kind of vessel he will be in the household of God. It is his choice to be a vessel of honor or dishonor. God is looking for a life that is clean and pure. Only then can that life be a vessel unto honor, sanctified to meet the master's use. Be perfected unto every good work.

CONCLUSION

To be a great and efficient leader is difficult, but with the combination of God's word, theological principals, and motivational theories, you can make strides. It is important that the church leader builds positive relationships with his members to help implement and model the church's vision for all.

References

Cable News Network. (2013). *CNN*. Retrieved August 8, 2021, from https://www.cnn.com/videos/us/2013/12/05/exp-lead-intv-rick-warren-faith-weight-loss.cnn.

Carraher, S. (2015). Signaling intelligence, signaling THEORY, Project A, and excellent management history research. *Journal of Management History, 21*(2). https://doi.org/10.1108/jmh-02-2015-0007

Crabb, L. J. (2013). *Inside out*. NavPress.

Deutsch, M. (1973). *The resolution of conflict: Constructive and destructive processes*. Yale University Press.

Goldhaber, G. (1990). *Organizational communication*. WCB.

Gordon, J. (n.d.). *McClelland's acquired Needs theory-explainedJ*. The Business Professor, LLC. Retrieved July 11, 2021, from https://thebusinessprofessor.com/management-leadership-organizational-behavior/acquired-need-theory-definition.

Holman Bible Publishers. (1989). *The holy bible: Authorized king James Version*.

Kanungo, R. N., & Mendonca, M. (1996). *Ethical dimensions of leadership*. Sage.

Maxwell, J. C. (2019). *Leadershift: The 11 essential changes every leader must embrace.* HarperCollins Leadership, an imprint of HarperCollins.

McGregor, D., & Cutcher-Gershenfeld, J. E. (2008). *The human side of enterprise.* McGraw-Hill Professional.

Quick, T. L. (1988, July). Expectancy theory in five simple steps. *Training & Development Journal, 42*(7), 30+. https://link.gale.com/apps/doc/A6833643/AONE?u=anon~f3a8e05c&sid=googleScholar&xid=2ede80d9

Sande, K., & Johnson, K. (2008). *The peacemaker student edition: Handling conflict without fighting back or running away.* Baker Books.

Sanders, J. O. (2017). *Spiritual leadership: Principles of excellence for every believer.* Moody Publishers.

Vroom, V. H., & Jago, A. G. (1988). *The new leadership: Managing participation in organizations.* Prentice Hall.

Vroom, V. H., & Yetton, P. W. (2017). *Leadership and decision-making.* University of Pittsburgh Press.

Wei, L. T., & Yazdanifard, R. (2014). The impact of positive reinforcement on employees' performance in organizations. *American Journal of Industrial and Business Management, 04*(01), 9–12. https://doi.org/10.4236/ajibm.2014.41002